The Calling

The Calling

Master Getting and Giving in the World of Work

ALICE ELIZABETH BING

ISBN: 1517659981
ISBN 13: 9781517659981
Library of Congress Control Number: 2016901799
CreateSpace Independent Publishing Platform
North Charleston, South Carolina

To my beloved Alyssa Bing, Leatrice Bulls, David Jenkins II, Derek Jenkins, Isaiah Hanley, and Aaron Hanley: make your living make a difference. To my father and mother: thank you for giving me the gift of feeling loved.

Acknowledgments

I am grateful to my husband, Moses Lee Bing, for his display of tremendous patience during the entire writing process. He demonstrated great sensibility toward my work motivations and preferences. His receptive disposition was unwavering.

A million thanks go to the individuals who talked with me or provided written feedback on the first rough draft: Sandra A. Chamber, associate dean of student affairs, Jefferson Community & Technical College; Knikeya Robinson, owner of Memorable Moments Massage LLC; Carla Bailey, owner of USA Background Incorporated; Lolita Hanley, real estate broker; and Tracy Alls, a former DUMP Furniture Store colleague.

I am sincerely grateful for the inspiration of three people who are no longer with us. Pam Sullivan's support, motivation, enthusiasm, and immense interest in the work I do are forever present. Terry Scott's advice helped me to rescue the best things about me from the jaws of destructive thinking. And my mother-in-law, Beatrice Bing, taught me that all I need to know is inside me.

I appreciate that my friend and former DUMP Furniture Store colleague John Wilson insisted I press on. He never put limits on his willingness to support me. He was not fooling around when he said, "If you need encouragement at two a.m., call me."

My sincere thanks also go out to Karen Bailey, CEO at Resource King International, LLC, for reaching out to me in response to an article I posted on LinkedIn. I also thank her for remembering my interest in writing. Karen wrote to me and said, "You're ready for your book!" She gave me great cause to ask myself when I would write this book if not now and to question why if I never did.

I am grateful illiteracy and stage freight I fought decades to end, did not derail my career motivation and preference to help people be happy at work. Without willingness to err on the side of audacity than fail by doing nothing, this book would have been impossible to write and speak about.

Contents

Introduction

My biggest motivation for lending a helping hand to workers is based on my belief that the world of work is an ideal station for gaining self-fulfillment, and once a person's deepest desires and capacities are being realized, making a difference by giving to others is certain to happen. I was able to make firm steps in the path of my motivation and come into the scope of its beauty by way of determination, self-discipline, and examinations of social science studies of work and satisfaction, philosophies of work, and personal stories of work.

An observation about the value of work made by Thomas Carlyle moved me. He remarked: "He that can work is born king of something." Carlyle lived between 1795 and 1881 and was a Scottish philosopher, satirical writer, essayist, historian and teacher. He was considered one of the most important social commentators of his time.

Hearing people's stories of regret touched me too. Their sadness drove me to think only about how I could help workers fulfill becoming kings of something. What I could not get out of my head were comments such as these:

"I wish I had heard your ideas earlier."

"You need to talk to those just starting out."

"Everyone needs to hear this stuff."

"I hated working there, but stayed for the money"

Having ideas for achieving happiness at work later rather than sooner is better than never having them at all, but being in possession of sustainable ways to be happy at work when just starting out or in the middle of a career is ideal. Methods for doing work continue to undergo tremendous change. But many workers are relying still on substances of work for inner happiness. Such substances of work are paycheck, promotion, work station, job title, flexible schedule, new job, new boss, and benefit package.

This book is of ideas I'm convinced plenty of workers will find reliable for enabling inner happiness during times of hardship at work. Everything in this book is based on my belief that every person engaging in work is being summoned to adhere to what I call the "ancient calling pertaining to work." Every working person is being asked to adhere to a request that has been in existence for a long time. I'm persuaded the ancient calling pertaining to work is a beckoning for a person to elevate involvement in work to an act of service for self and others.

We stand to lose too much *joy* by not aiming to serve ourselves and others through the world of work. Yet very possible by aiming to do both, keeping steps firm, and making attitude adjustments timely, we stand to gain much *joy*. Believing the calling is real will magnetize ideas we need to answer the calling. Persistence toward developing talents and skills will prepare us to fashion our ideas into tools for improving ourselves and others. Through self-determination to err on the side of audacity than fail by doing nothing, will enable us to achieve the purpose for going to work: the point is to gain food, water, warmth, rest, fulfillment, and help others prosper personally, physically, socially, economically, and intellectually. I call that *getting and giving in the world of work*. With every fiber of my being, I intent to enable people to experience joy that flows from doing the getting-giving thing.

Author Ralph Waldo Emerson wrote, "Unless you try to do something beyond what you have already mastered, you will never grow." Because we are persuaded that going to work to make a living is in our best interest, and since we're born with the inclination to improve self and others, we have what it takes to answer the calling. This book's sole purpose is to help you and others seek, sense, and select ideas that can help to merge at work serving self and others without uncalled-for difficulty.

The great Michelangelo once said, "The greatest danger for most of us lies not in setting our aim too high and falling short, but in setting our aim too low, and achieving our mark." You and others want nothing more than to satisfy your yearning to do the whole of what you feel you are meant to do with the earthly time you've been given. The human spirit of self-determination is amazing. It's true. People would rather err on the side of audacity than fail by doing nothing. Because people are willing to go to work to make a living, and since at work most of us are unable to turn off the feeling of wanting fulfillment, this book is also about preparing people to gain satisfaction.

Groups from Harvard University and Gallup Inc. have released tremendous documents that show that people believe work and joy go hand in hand. So this book is also about helping working people enhance their abilities to live what they feel and believe in. The ideas in this book are not confined to a period of time. They are portable and can facilitate transformation, so adult professional can refer to them for progressing through his or her career journey.

My inspiration for reaching out to the whole workforce is also rooted in my belief that going to work to gain food, water, warmth, rest, fulfillment, as well as to make the world a better place is a piece of the puzzle for happiness in life. Consider a statement made by the thirteenth-century theologian and philosopher Thomas Aquinas: "There can be no joy in living without joy in work, because much of our living is about work." This book, then, is also about preparing working people to gain joy in living through joy in work.

Most of us are certain to agree with Thomas Aquinas's thinking about the relationship between joy in work and joy in living. In spite of that it is reasonable to wonder whether making a living by doing the getting-giving thing is the purpose of work or just a fantasy. It is wise to ask whether what I am speaking of is truth or delusion. What is truth, though? I am satisfied with Paul Pardi's answer: "Truth, like knowledge, is surprisingly difficult to define because as soon as you think you have it pinned down, some case or counterexample immediately shows deficiencies." Because truth is in the eye of the beholder, I say humbly that truth is equivalent to the earth's sun. Clouds, rain, and earth's rotations are not consequential. The sun stays put and shines brightly during all three episodes. I am convinced that thinking the purpose of work is about something other than getting what is needed and giving what is needed is simply a misunderstanding. I also proclaim that a misunderstanding can only cloud the mind from seeing truth. It cannot change truth.

I encourage everyone to investigate whether the sole purpose of work is to use talents to get what is needed and to give what is needed. I included in my investigation my observations of centuries of human interactions, documentations of working people who wanted their work to fit with their senses of personal purpose, and philosophical, scientific, ancient, and contemporary views about work.

Widely known empirical data and informal information corroborate that the time in which the majority of workers believed happiness at work is a luxury not a necessity is passing away. No wonder fewer members of the workforce are willing to accept the concept that work is not personal. All people need to feel that the work they do fits with who they are. They also need to feel that the people with whom they work are friendly and respectful toward every member of the organization. Today, workers of traditional and baby boomer generations see the importance of pleasure at work the same as X, Y, and Z generations of workers. They feel contentment at work is essential to having it over-all. All generations of workers currently in the workplace are seekers of inner joy. That excites me. We all prefer a happy restaurant cook over one hating his or her job. Everyone favors workers under the influence of *inner* happiness.

Earlier generations of workers pursuing "second act" careers are unwilling to trade contentment for a paycheck or promotion. Today's workers are not going to adhere to the old idea of fake happiness to have materials of work. They are sensitive to the negative consequences of trying to find happiness in substances of work. I wrote this book also because I'm convinced they are right to not place happiness at work on the sideline. Joy of working in the heart is likening to that jolt of power charging an engine. Oh, the wonderful places you'll go and help others reach with joy of working in your heart.

It is not by chance that humans possess a natural mechanism for transitioning successfully into getting-giving at work. Once people have few or no worries about their physical safety and security, they are able to facilitate actualization and extend helping hands. The human desire to reach out is nondiscriminatory. As a result, people respond to opportunities to help at home, in neighborhoods, through community entities, and in workplaces.

I am passionate about aiding every working person's progress toward making a difference for self and others through occupations. I'm influenced by my belief that the work institution is an area of life responsible for the care of people and our home, the earth. I hope the ideas in this book help thousands of working people to experience the world of work as an awesome gift, and I hope they are helped to stretch to do something better, something new, and the things they believe they are meant to do.

Humans are always in need of ideas that can help them improve their thinking and doing. It's a good thing humans are skilled at gathering the things they need. The ideas between the covers of this book are meant to bring to plenty workers the joy of serving self and others through workplaces.

One

WHAT IS WORK?

Transferred Energy

The physics community and the religious community have concluded that work is transferred energy on an object. Both have declared essentially that to know what work is, you have to see what is beyond work. In the world of physics, work is done on an object when a person transfers energy to that object. A person's work on an object can travel to intended and unintended objects. Here is an illustration of transferred energy: if one object transfers energy to another object, then the first object does work on the second object.

The following are views of work according to some religious leaders. Thirteenth-century theologian Thomas Aquinas said that work is "to display a good activity." The elaboration on Aquinas's view of work by Episcopal priest and author Matthew Fox elucidates this view. Fox said, "Work is part of our display, part of the parading of our beauty. It is the way we return our beauty to the community. This is important both to the individual and to the community, because all beauty yearns to be conspicuous." Another of Fox's thoughts on Aquinas's view of work is seen in his statement, "Our work is meant to be beautiful, to increase the beauty of the world, of one another, of the worker." I took Fox's quotes from his book *The Reinvention of Work: A New Vision of Livelihood for Our Time*. This book displays the purpose of work in a very complete fashion. It's the most comprehensive piece about the purpose of work I've studied to date.

Fox's views bring to mind the Bible verse found in Matthew 5:14: "Ye are the light of the world. A city that is set on a hill cannot be hid. Neither do men light a candle and put it under a bushel but on a candlestick. It gives light unto all that are in the house."

Before the time of Thomas Aquinas, the twelfth-century Benedictine abbess Hildegard of Bingen delivered an astonishing notion about work. She stressed that "when humans do good work, they become flowering orchards permeating the universe and making the cosmic wheel turn." It's in doing *good work* that *good* sprout and spread. Believing must be the first movement toward answering *the calling*. The second must be something encouraged by Baha'u'llah, a divine educator and founder of the Baha'i faith. "He urged people to learn and practice arts, trades, crafts, or professions for the good of themselves, their families, and society as a whole. He called for each person to do such things to the highest possible level of proficiency, beauty, and service."

If transferred energy on one and perhaps several objects is the reality of work, then, we should contemplate each time possible consequences before transferring energy onto people, animals, earth, or machinery. Henry Brooks Adams, an American historian and member of the Adams political family, being descended from two U.S. Presidents, had a saying: "A teacher affects eternity; he can never tell where his influence stops."

A Process for Human Nobility

Work is simply one of many things willed into existence to provide humanity ways to live majestically. Like the experiences of family and community living, work is bittersweet and full of ups and downs. Each person is accountable for employing personal capabilities to hold up the intention of work to cause living nobly. To keep your mind from becoming too overwhelmed by workplace stresses, do a daily practice of transitioning the mind away from thinking of work as something to avoid, a punishment, necessary evil, curse, and any other concepts not extoling the virtues of work. In place of such ideas, define work as an *act of service*. Thinking of work as a grand opportunity to serve you and others does require a change in thoughts, feelings, ideas, and perceptions. Taking a daily account of your actions at work using these four accountability questions will help ease this shift: Am I supplying myself things I need to have a fulfilling journey? Am I matching what I know to what people need? Am I helping to identify problems and solve them? Am I causing the state of affairs to improve?

Even though you will not like all your job assignments, never allow that to become your excuse for not making good service your mission. Consider Ralph Waldo Emerson's words of wisdom: "Don't waste life in doubts and fears; spend yourself on the work before you, well assured that the right performance of the hour's duties will be the best preparation for the hours and ages that will follow it."

Regardless of the job assignments you have, always stay in love with presenting extraordinary work. When all is said and done, what remains are the ways you have influenced others. Consider how you want people to feel about what you do. Never allow simply having a job to be your hope. Hope also to make a difference. Unpleasant circumstances in the world of work are real. Yet, within your control is your ability to figure out how to progress under various working conditions.

While watching the movie *Iron Lady*, I became keenly aware of something else you can do to facilitate fulfillment and making a difference in life through your job. I urge you to stay away from developing the "what's in it for me" (WIFM) attitude. In the film, Meryl Streep, who played Prime Minister Margaret Thatcher, said, "It used to be about trying to do something. Now it's about trying to be someone." That brings to mind this well-known quote: "My fellow Americans, ask not what your country can do for you, ask what you can do for your country." President John F. Kennedy is credited with making those remarks in his inaugural address in 1961.

Keep this in mind: good deeds make you a remarkable person. Staying away from the WIFM attitude will help you focus on doing meaningful things in your job. Going forward, begin to labor as though you are convinced your professional calling is to help the world become a better place for people. Embrace working as one of several processes for gaining human nobility. There are certainly downsides to working, but there are also plenty of opportunities to succeed at making a living and making a difference. Walter E. Cole said,

"We must look for opportunities in every difficulty instead of being paralyzed at the thought of the difficulty in every opportunity."

Presentation

Think about the task of extracting gold from rock. Four major jobs or tasks must be performed for the gold to become separated from the rock. The first is removing the gold-bearing rock from the ground. The second is starting the process of isolating the pure gold by breaking down large chucks of rock into smaller pieces the size of road gravel. The third is applying a process that can grind the rock to a fine slurry or powder. The fourth is thickening the slurry with water to form a pulp and then running the pulp through a series of filtering tanks designed to dissolve the gold out of the rock using a chemical solvent. Once the gold is extracted, the task is now complete. The removed gold is a splendid presentation of someone's work. I declare work to be a splendid presentation, to be what St. Thomas Aquinas described as a "display of a good activity" or what Matthew Fox spoke of as "part of the parading of our beauty."

Grand Opportunity

As pointed out previously, work is a grand opportunity for people to act on the desire to make the world a better place. There is a combination of favorable conditions for you to make a difference in life through work. Things giving you that chance are the time you have, the skills you already possess and can develop, the networks you have built, the collaborations you can form, the visions you can put forth, the procedures you can influence, the perspectives you can voice, the planning you can do, and the needs people have that you can learn about.

What Making a Difference from the Workplace Looks Like:

- Communicative activities are being used to facilitate quality and quantity input.
- Bold new ways to ensure the education of all children are growing.

- Businesses are focused only on what can uplift humanity.
- Information and technology are improving everyday life for all people.
- Wellness strategies and better health-care solutions are underway.
- Affordable and environmentally friendly energy resources are not uncommon.
- Emphasis is being placed on making fundamental foods affordable.
- Focus is being placed on the building of a society that values all people.
- Practical money management lessons are helping people live better.
- The growing elderly population is becoming well integrated into society.
- Family, community, social, and work activities are in support of each other.
- Priority is being given to the mentally ill and drug-addicted members of society.
- Youth and young adults are learning life skills for living in a global society.
- Community architectural designs are supporting recreational and social needs.
- Foods are being introduced for physical and hormonal well-being.
- Focus is on education, job opportunities, and rehabilitation.

Two

PHILOSOPHIES OF WORK

Are the striking similarities of the philosophies of work described in this chapter coincidental or evidence of something factual? Consider this: people of varying personal and vocational backgrounds living hundreds of years apart have declared that work is another path to happiness in life.

St. Thomas Aquinas, 1225–74

Earlier I mentioned St. Thomas Aquinas, a thirteenth-century Catholic priest in the Dominican Order. He pointed out that "to live well is to work well, to show a good activity." Because Aquinas arrived at his viewpoints by way of observations using his mind and his senses, he was opposed by those who struggled to reconcile the relationship between theology (faith) and philosophy (reasoning). Based on Averroes's "theory of double truth," the two types of knowledge are in opposition to each other. Aquinas's position was that "both kinds of knowledge ultimately come from God" and are, therefore, compatible and can work in collaboration. He pointed out that revelation can guide reason and prevent it from making mistakes, while reason can clarify and demystify faith.

Ralph Waldo Emerson, 1803-1882

Ralph Waldo Emerson is known for regarding the process of reasoning as the key to the knowledge of spiritual reality. This is called transcendentalism. As a champion of individualism, he is known for emphasizing that intuition is a means of knowing a spiritual reality. In other words, humans can know a spiritual reality without actual evidence for it. Intuition is the ability to know or understand things without any proof or evidence.

Emerson's way of thinking is worth sharing because each of us can do a much better job of not allowing fears and doubts to consume the knowledge of how a vocation can make a difference. Consider this quote from Emerson: "Don't waste life in doubts and fears; spend yourself on the work before you, well assured that the right performance of the hour's duties will be the best preparation for the hours and ages that will follow it." I imagine Emerson as an individual who took painstaking steps to encourage people to think for themselves. Reflect on another quote of his: "To be yourself in a world that is constantly trying to make you something else is the greatest accomplishment."

Thomas Alva Edison, 1847-1931

Holding a world record of 1,093 patents for inventions must have influenced Thomas Alva Edison to proclaim that "opportunity is missed by most because it is dressed in coveralls and looks like work."

Edison's inventions are tremendous in number, and they greatly influence life around the world today. His inventions include but are not limited to the phonograph, the motion picture camera, and the long-lasting practical light bulb. He also helped to apply the principle of mass production and to create the first industrial laboratory. Some widespread results of Edison's inventions are electric lights, utilities, sound recordings, and motion pictures. This statement of Edison signifies his attitude toward work: "I never perfected an invention that I didn't think of in terms of the service it might give others. I find out what the world needs, then I proceed to invent it."

W. E. B. DuBois, 1868-1963

W. E. B. DuBois, the American sociologist, historian, civil rights activist, Pan-Africanist, author, and editor, fought to empower black Americans of his day to live well and strive to do better. While growing up in the mostly European American town of Great Barrington, Massachusetts, William Edward Burkhardt, better known as W. E. B. DuBois, attended school with whites and was strongly supported in his academics by his white teachers. DuBois's understanding of black life in the South came into view in 1885 while traveling to Nashville, Tennessee, to attend Fisk University. In his travels, Jim Crow laws met him at various southern borders. The awakening thrust him into studying the deep troubles of US racism. In the face of widespread racial hatred, he earned his bachelor's degree from Fisk, entered Harvard University, completed a master's degree there, and then became the first African American to earn a PhD from Harvard. DuBois's recognition of black life in the southern states and his unshakable interest in justice for black Americans affected the remainder of his life.

Two of DuBois's quotes about work include the following:

"The return from your work must be the satisfaction that work brings you and the world's need of that work. With this, life is heaven, or as near heaven as you can get. Without this — with work which you despise, which bores you, and which the world does not need — this life is hell."

"The worker must work for the glory of his handiwork, not simply for pay; the thinker must think for truth, not for fame."

Helen Keller, 1880-1968

Helen Keller lived at a time when blind and deaf people were rarely escorted into public arenas. Rather, they spent their days tucked away in their living quarters. The blind and deaf Keller, however, became an American author, political activist, and lecturer. She also became known as the first blind and deaf person in the United States to earn a bachelor of arts. Keller demonstrated belief in her ability to make a living for herself and to contribute to the livelihoods of others. Keller said, "I long to accomplish a great and noble task, but it is my chief duty to accomplish humble tasks as though they were great and noble. The world is moved along, not only by the mighty shoves of its heroes, but also by the aggregate of the tiny pushes of each honest worker."

Even though Keller spent forty-four years working with the American Foundation for the Blind, that work never occupied the center of her identity. Her sympathies were with all who struggled for justice. Whether or not you agree with her politics, Keller's courage was indisputable. She opposed racism. She was also an early feminist who spoke out for the rights of women to get an education and to work. She was an advocate for birth control. Keller was one of the first to criticize the horrors of the Holocaust, and her disapproval led to the Nazis burning her books. At a time when unions were even less popular than they are now, Keller advocated for the labor movement.

Marian Wright Edelman, 1939–

Children's Defense Fund founder Marian Wright Edelman became known for her commitment to fight for the rights of children. She established the Children's Defense Fund in 1973 for disadvantaged children and families. Being a champion for any social cause is not easy. Hard work and endurance are required to get politicians to take a serious look at the Children's Defense Fund agenda. The organization pushes for policies and programs that lift America's children out of poverty, protect them from abuse and neglect, and ensure their access to health care, quality education, and a moral and spiritual foundation.

Edelman states that "we must not, in trying to think about how we can make a big difference, ignore the small daily differences we can make which, over time, add up to big differences that we often cannot foresee."

Alexandra Stoddard, 1967–

The following definition of work comes from interior designer and lifestyle philosopher Alexandra Stoddard: "Work is an opportunity to bring something forth—to create something, complete something, invent something authentic and original."

Stoddard's aim is to bring to light the small but significant things that we can do to change our attitude, heart and environment for the better. The rare opportunity she had at sixteen years old enhanced her vocation. Under the supervision of her aunt, Ruth Elizabeth Johns, a renowned international social worker, she took a trip around the world. That trip exposed her to architecture, design, and beauty as well as to sorrow and suffering. In a nutshell, the tour taught her that we should do all within our power to end up on a path toward greater inner peace and lasting happiness.

Three

WORK AND QUALITY OF LIFE

No Work

Mastering getting and giving in the world of work is a good thing. What might be the fate of a society without labor? Imagine that tomorrow—throughout the world—every employee and all community volunteers are without work. Picture the impact that would have on you, your family, and the more than seven billion people living in the world. Can you see the numerous miseries that would be associated with the absence of labor? There would be no water, food, comfort, relief, medical attention, security, or safety, and we would all miss the helping hands of caring community volunteers.

Labor is what keeps water clean and running, food safe and available, power up and flowing, emergency services ready, law enforcement protecting, family and community life stable, and government services to citizens in place. If labor ceased for just twenty-four hours, thousands to millions of lives would expire. Plenty of people would face suffering too great to conceive.

Second-Rate Work

The scenario imagined isn't likely to happen. But incompetent labor can make daily living harder for people. To labor intelligently, the first order of business is to identify the needs. Then choose the best remedies. As explained in chapter 1, work is done on an object when a person transfers energy to that object. Everyone has had the experience of dealing with a person's or organization's poor or intelligent handling of a situation. The quality of your livelihood depends first on your labor. Then it depends on the labor of thinkers, researchers, collaborators, organizers, planners, nurses, doctors, teachers, financial planners, builders, law enforcers, sanitation workers, custodians, farmers, managers, supervisors, inventors, politicians, military branches, non-profit organizations, faith-based groups, food handlers, citizens, counselors, and many other people in pivotal paid and non-paid positions.

By each laborer doing what makes a difference, benevolence spreads from person to person. "By virtue of exchange, one man's prosperity is beneficial to all others," said early free-market economist and classical French author C. F. Bastiat. This expresses clearly how we flourish, thrive, and have good fortune. As Helen Keller observed, human affairs are moved from poor to good "by the tiny pushes of each honest worker." Another worthwhile thought about work came from leader of the civil rights movement Martin Luther Kings, Jr. He said, "All labor that uplifts humanity has dignity and importance and should be undertaken with painstaking excellence."

Dispirited Work

Sadder, more prevalent, and more influential than second-rate labor is dispirited labor. A hands-off approach toward work is much more harmful than is an incompetent one. Because the noninterventionist attitude toward work derives from a feeling of apathy, it is lethal. The apathetic feeling toward work can show up dressed as lack of interest.

The plane on which dispirited labor rests is different from that of second-rate labor. All that is usually required to move to first-rate labor from second-rate or even third-rate labor is for people to be willing to step up to home plate and hit the ball in good form.

Apathetic feelings should be taken seriously. Apathy is defined as the absence of emotion and can grow into full-blown depression. If you or someone you know is unable to improve perspective and outlook, please consult with a competent professional.

Listed below are possible negative results of apathy on the apathetic person. People overtaken by apathy cannot benefit themselves or others. Apathy can do the following:

- Destroy visionary ability, leaving the person dreamless and void of ideas.
- Impede energy, leaving the person unable to think clearly.
- Block talents, leaving the person with a sense of worthlessness.
- Hinder learning, leaving the person incompetent.
- Obstruct self-determination, leaving the person dependent.

Lack of Work

A poor economy, lack of preparation to work, and social injustice are the biggest and most likely causes of unemployment in any society. Since attainment of personal livelihood and the greatest opportunities to help a person are linked to working, lack of opportunity for employment can crush a person's sense of worth. By all accounts, people want to take advantage of the special opportunities in the world of work through applications of their gifts and talents. No elaborate explanation is required for us to understand the spiritually devastating results of lack of work. Adequate participation in the world of work can give a big boost to one's sense of pride, hope, and purpose.

There is no question why insufficient participation in the labor market leads to despair. When people feel dejected, see no light at the end of the tunnel, and lose heart with mainstream society, they might feel no other choice but to act in ways unbecoming of good citizens. Also, people who lack control over their livelihoods have more debilitating health issues. Once hope fades, only meaningful work opportunities can restore hope.

My focus on the influences of a lack of labor caused me to think about two others quotes from Thomas Carlyle. He said this in his inaugural address as rector of the University of Edinburgh in Edinburgh, Scotland, on April

2, 1866: "The most unhappy of all men is the man who cannot tell what he is going to do, who has got no work cut-out for him in the world, and does not go into it, for work is the grand cure of all the maladies and miseries that ever beset mankind,—honest work, which you intend getting done." Another relevant expression of Carlyle's is this: "A man willing to work, and unable to find work, is perhaps the saddest sight that fortune's [affluence's] inequality exhibits under the sun."

Four

BECOMING A BENEFICIARY AND BENEFACTOR OF IDEAS

Since all people involved in working need useful returns on the investments they're making in the world of work, everyone should make giving-and-taking of ideas a time-honored event. In this section are details of the relationship between sense of belongingness and motivation to engage in exchange of ideas. Also are the models I created to help individuals learn how to facilitate exchange of ideas in the workplace or elsewhere.

What individuals and organizations are missing by not making give-and-take of ideas a standard practice is profound. As C. F. Bastiat expressed, "By virtue of exchange, one man's prosperity is beneficial to all others." This book would be incomplete without pieces of others in it. By advantage of millions of years of idea exchanging, this book became possible. As I am writing, I can feel the presence of those whom I have never met but have come to appreciate for the superb literature they left behind. As I am writing, I am taking in the encouraging words of family, friends, and colleagues who have passed through this material world. I am a beneficiary of their prosperities.

American psychologist, teacher, and writer Dr. Allan Fromme emphasized that "people have been known to achieve more as a result of working with others than against them." Human beings do not thrive when isolated from what other people know and can do. That is the meaning of the following line from John Donne, who lived between 1572 and 1631. "No man is an island, entire of self; every man is a piece of the continent, a part of the main."

The four things you should try to learn about a person are precisely the things a person would like for you to learn. Because most of us are sensitive to looking like braggers, our worthwhile stories go untold. We want those around us to know the things we value most about the work we do, things we feel we are doing well, things we would like to initiate, and things we want to influence. Our need to be known is purposeful. We want people to know how we see ourselves fitting in and contributing. If our stories are not heard, then, we will lack a satisfied sense of belongingness. If we lack sense of belongingness, as a consequence, we will lack motivation to engage in give-and-take processes.

Feeling free to tell our stories can improve our sense of belongingness, and that can motivate us to engage in the sharing and receiving of ideas. To me the need to feel safe when sharing fits Psychologist Abraham Maslow category of safety needs that includes things such as protection from elements, security, order, law, stability, and freedom from fear. If people don't feel safe in speaking up, there valuable stories will go untold. Consequently, others will be less well-off.

The need to belong is part of what makes us human. We can never outgrow it. We cannot achieve compartmentalizing our need for sense of belongingness to only areas outside of work. A common definition of belongingness is this: It's a human need to be an accepted member of a group. Many psychologists say we have an inherent desire to belong and be an important part of something greater than ourselves. That means we desire a relationship that is greater than simple acquaintance or familiarity. And so, the need to belong is the need to be giving and be given unto.

As workers we come together in workplaces. That is our beginning. We stay together for a period. That is our continuance. We exchange ideas. That is our success. We must avoid making the mistake of underestimating the power of a sense of being in the right place, fitting in, being suitable, and being relevant. There is no way for anyone to leave the need to belong outside of the workplace. People welcome meaningful attention. Asking about things people wish for you to know carries great weight. That can inspire people to give and receive great ideas. That can rev up a sense of belongingness at work.

My purpose for creating and placing the four modules in this section is to help you make inquiries into the four areas that are important to people working to make a living. Integrating the questions in each module into one-on-one conversations and group conversations can make the discussions much more fluent, fruitful, and fun. Adding in self-disclosure can encourage people to open up.

Questions such as the ones in Module A can help ascertain what the person values most about the work he or she does. When the person feels that his or her values are appreciated, he or she is now more psychologically prepared to respond to the job in an all-embracing manner.

Module A

You're such an energetic worker; what's driving you?

You seem excited; what's going on?

How do you feel about that service/product?

What would you say was the best part of yesterday's workday?

How would you like customers to feel about our business?

Which of yesterday's events would you like to reminisce about?

What are you enjoying most about the assignment?

What would you say are the best parts of your job?

Say you have free rein to do more of the things you enjoy doing. Which things would you choose?

What would you say customers value most about the work you do?

What satisfies you most about your job?

What would you like for customers to say about the work you do?

How do you like to surprise customers?

What impressions do you like to leave with customers?

What was your most memorable moment last week?

Of your job duties, which one or ones would you gladly do more often?

Questions such as the ones in Module B can help you ascertain what the person is doing well. Feeling good about what is going well inspires the person to stretch toward doing well overall.

Module B

Wow! How did you accomplish that?

Explain how you did that.

Tell me how you solved that problem.

How did he, she, or they react to what you did?

I'm curious. How did you solve that problem?

What information brought you to that conclusion?

What would you like to tackle next? What is your plan for achieving that?

That's great! How did you arrive at that solution?

You handled that well! How did you do that?

How can you take that achievement to the next level?

What did you have to overcome to accomplish that?

That turned out better! What did you do differently?

How did you have so much confidence in that approach?

Questions such as the ones in Module C can help you ascertain what the person has self-determination to do. The more the person sees that he or she is an initiator of something, the more likely the person is to take greater advantage of the freedom he or she has to initiate things.

Module C

What are your options?

What have you tried so far?

Presume you have free rein. What would you do?

Which of the tasks is next on your agenda?

What do you think should be the next step?

Do you have any tips?

What do you want the outcome to be?

How would you like me to assist you?

What daily routine works best for you?

What adjustments can you make to achieve that goal?

What do you intend to do?

What work pace should you be aiming for?

Who can help you get that done?

Where are the bottlenecks for you? How can you overcome them?

How can you make that happen?

What do you think could help the customer feel satisfied?

What can you do to be even more effective?

Questions such as the ones in Module D can help you ascertain the positive impacts a person is making. Every person has earned some bragging rights. When you invite the person to talk about the positive impacts he or she made, you have granted the person permission to celebrate and appreciate good work done. By doing that, you are influencing the person to do more to make a difference.

Module D

Do you realize how what you did made a difference?

What do you think would have occurred had you not stepped up?

How is the work you are doing making a difference?

That was effective. Do you grasp the difference you just made?
Time to celebrate! Which accomplishments would you like to share?
Thanks for doing that. How did he, she, or they respond to what you did?
Toot your horn! Which accomplishments are you most proud of?
What did you do to cause that to turn out so well?
What a milestone! How do you feel about your progress?
Do you realize you exceeded the expectations?
What would have happened if you had not accomplished that?

Five

WORKING OR WORKED?

*A*re you working, or are you worked? I define "working" as being in a state of mind to elevate involvement in work to the level of service. "Worked" is being in a state of mind to no more than take home paychecks, do as much as necessary so not to get fired, have off days, or try to retire on the job. If you are in the state of being worked, you can evolve from there to the state of working. Take a moment to reexamine my description of the ancient calling pertaining to work: Every working person is being asked to develop talents and skills needed to acquire food, water, warmth, rest, fulfillment, *and* to help others prosper personally, physically, socially, economically, and intellectually.

What I mean by *rest*: It's more than ending a work day, finishing a work week, taking a vacation, or retiring. It's having memorable moments to reflect at any time you choose. Forget trying to retire on the job. That's as difficult as aiming to stand still in the middle of a crowd coming at you from all directions. To do as much as necessary so not to get fired is equivalent to being that person in a Dodgeball game ducting constantly in hope of not getting hit by the flung ball.

At times workers simply must try extra hard to have warm fuzzy feelings at work. That's extremely true in cases of lack of job fit, lack of variation, lack of social appreciation for the job, and lack of sense of making an impact. The saddest cases of unhappiness at work are those lasting most of or the entire career journey. A retired worker earning a sustainable retirement check from a Global Fortune 500 company told me he hated every day of the decades he worked at that company. Hate is a deep and emotional extreme dislike. It can be directed against individuals, groups, entities, objects, behaviors, or ideas. He used the word several times to describe his feeling toward working there. Paycheck, life insurance, and company retirement plan are three ways to comprehend why he, you, or someone else might become motivated to tolerate decades of unhappiness. But understanding how little to no awareness of one's inner motivations and preferences for work can single-handedly entangle a person in unhappiness, is more important to know. You can study fine points of *motivations and preferences* for work in chapter 8 of this book.

Why you shouldn't spend time at work not knowing about and working within your motivations and preferences for work? Even though from time-to-time I needed a pick-me-upper, *happy* is how I spent my days as a substitute teacher. The happiness I experienced resulted from the strong fit between my career aspiration and the job of facilitating learning by adhering to established rules and by employing workable ideas with the intent to ensure a wholesome learning environment.

Because facilitating learning is a job I'm highly motivated to do in the world of work, and my preference in a school system is to work with high-schoolers, my sense of belongingness stayed elevated. But when a student's interest was elsewhere, I had to exert extra attempts to enjoy the work that I'm highly motivated to do. I had to adjust every so often my attitude toward a student behaving badly so not to paint any student with a broad brush. Many times I had to tweak how I was going about trying to acquire students' buy-in towards the creation of a happy classroom environment. By doing such things, my desire to help each student to have more chances of becoming enlightened individuals was often achieved.

There were no dull days. Once a high school student able to be well-mannered yelled, "May I go to the bathroom I need to poop." Laughs broke out. I had to breathe deeply in order to respond not in kind. At the right moment privately, I said to the student next time try to not display publicly your exact need. The student replied softly and sweetly "ok". Most students complied right away. But just one student acting not in accordance to school etiquettes could interrupt learning for every student. That student might be only taking advantage of the substitute teacher situation or having a bad day. At the thought of having to call upon an administrator to intervene due to a disruptive classroom behavior made me uncomfortable. Achieving students' buy-in was my goal. So I challenged constantly myself to think up ways to accomplish my aim often. The pay-offs were fewer students off course, a boost to my career objective to facilitate learning, and a profound increase in my ability to be imaginative.

To help yourself over-come feeling work, consider a suggested by His Holiness the Dalai Lama. Author of *The Art of Happiness at Work* by Howard C. Cutler, M. D. presented a question related to feeling worked to His Holiness the Dalai Lama. Recorded on page 19 in the book is this answer: "They still have other kinds of choices in terms of their attitudes, how they interact with their co-workers, whether they utilize certain inner qualities or spiritual strengths to change their attitude at work even though the nature of the work may be difficult."

Making a few small changes can make a big difference. Don't suffer in silence. A therapist or psychologist can help you make decisions and clarify your feelings. A career coach can help you plan and manage your career. Look around for an experienced and trusted adviser to mentor you. To improve your sense of psychological empowerment at work, try a few things such as becoming better efficient at doing a task, reaching out to assist others, solving a small problem of the organization, or helping to create a welcoming environment.

An excellent example of choosing a different attitude or boosting sense of self value takes place every day at Pike Place Fish Market located in Seattle, Washington. People come from all over the world to see their world famous crew of fishmongers throwing fish and having fun with customers and to buy fantastic seafood they can have shipped home. To see the fishmongers having fun, visit them at www.pikeplacefish.com.

How much you are able to transition to the "working" mind-set depends on how much you believe in the calling and your enthusiasm to fight to live it. There are always going to be stressful circumstances of work, such as personality conflicts, internal and external demands, work overload, demanding hours, low pay, learning challenges, lack of advancement opportunities, and travel to and from the workplace. Only you can provide yourself protection against situations that could cause you to go against your natural desire to use your talents to infuse that which is good.

Unpleasant aspects of work, if left unmanaged, will cause you to fumble in the world of work. This is true even of the person who has sharp job skills and sincere intentions to make a difference and to achieve great things. Making good use of talents and intentions is no easy task. Negative events might not outnumber positive opportunities, but they are bothersome. Here is the good news: the more perturbed humans become, the more self-determination they summon. Since you accepted the job offer, take responsibility for using the job to make a difference. Consider the ideas below.

- Start every day with a simple question, who needs help and how can I help?
- Stay away from forming a scarcity mentality toward availability of methods.
- Take advantage of the organization's resources you can use to make a difference.
- Give away knowledge to all people who are good stewards of information.
- Build a sense of community and connection in your immediate surroundings and, if possible, at all levels.
- Pay attention to what you are already doing to make a difference and expand on that.
- Grow in knowledge and skills by doing your homework.

Let me share more about what I mean by "working." Working means to escape the trap of becoming worked. Turning your dream of becoming the contributor you imagine into reality is escaping the trap. It means to overcome things that can deflate your flight above the muddiness of work. It means to allow the ideas you value to live through you in workplaces. It means to set aside doubts and fears and to trust your instincts. It means becoming less likely to fumble your dreams and perhaps cause others to miss things for their well-being.

There is another way I explain my role in helping people rise above becoming "worked." I help people help themselves so they can help others. Things that excite me are people's drives to satisfy their need to extend helping hands, the endless opportunities for them to achieve that through their jobs, and the fact that people are opened to having fresh ideas.

Six

Developing and Maintaining the Working Mind-Set

If you're wondering whether all this counseling meant for preparing working people to achieve happiness at work is necessary, then, consider this point of view. Since most of your time in life will probably be spent working, work problems left unchecked can make nearly your whole life difficult, according to science. Alexander Kjerulf, the "Chief Happiness Officer" of Woohoo inc, and one of the world's leading experts on workplace happiness, wrote in the Huffington Post about the five major ways that hating your job can harm your health. They are as follows:

- Hating your job can make you gain weight.
- Hating your job can weaken your immune system.
- Hating your job can ruin your relationships.
- Hating your job can rob you of sleep.
- Hating your job increases your risk of serious illness.

The line separating the working mind-set and the worked mind-set is inconspicuous. It is like black ice on the road: you must stay alert to it. To do that, I recommend that you care for the working mind-set by concentrating on the things you find valuable about the work you are doing, the things you are doing well, the things you are determined to do, and the things that you are positively influencing.

To help you stay on track, I created activities designed to increase your ability to stay focused on the four things I just mentioned. I suggest you grab paper and pencil so that you can record your responses in a safe and retrievable place. Update them when necessary, and refer to them for self-validation. Use them to market your best self when undergoing a job performance evaluation, writing a résumé, or participating in a job interview.

To move toward developing and maintaining the working mind-set, concentrate on the things you value about the work you are doing by responding to the questions below.

A. If the influences of your work lasted forever, what influences would you like to leave behind?
B. If there are aspects of your job you value most, name a few of them.
C. If in your current job you have been characterized as a hard worker, give your opinion of how you earned that reputation.
D. If you have ever been deeply inspired by a person or an event at work, briefly describe the experience.
E. If you were given free rein in your job to do one special thing, what one thing would you choose to do?

To move toward developing and maintaining the working mind-set, concentrate on things you are doing well by responding to the questions below.

Instructions: Describe an important job duty you are performing well. Consider this job duty when answering questions A, B, C, and D.

A. Of the job skills you have, which ones are you using most to perform the job duty described?
B. What challenges have you had to overcome to be able to perform the job duty described?

C. If you believe you have other job skills you can start using in the job duty described, what are they?
D. How is your performance in the job duty causing you to be a valuable team player?

To move toward developing and maintaining the working mind-set, concentrate on the things you are determined to do by responding to the questions below.

Instructions: Describe a time when you initiated a solution to a problem. Consider this description when answering questions A, B, C, and D.

A. What solution did you initiate?
B. If you initiated input, whom was it from and why?
C. If a barrier was particularly difficult to overcome, what was it?
D. What do you feel was the most important outcome of all?

To move toward developing and maintaining the working mind-set, concentrate on the things you are influencing positively by responding to the questions below.

Instructions: If you have gone beyond the call of duty to make special things happen, you have created memorable and pleasurable moments. Describe what you think was one of those moments. Consider your description when answering questions A, B, C, and D.

A. Suppose you had not fortified your efforts in the above situation. What could have happened?
B. Describe the efforts you put forth to make a difference in that situation.
C. Describe the recipient's reaction at the end of that transaction.
D. Describe how you felt at the end of that transaction.

Seven

WORKING OUT THE EXPERIENCE YOU WANT

Be Prepared

As Sir William Osler indicated, "The best preparation for tomorrow is to do today's work." If you want to increase ways to make a living and do more to make a difference, then you need to focus each day on preventing problems by identifying and solving them. That's doing today's work. Preparation for tomorrow requires you to not slip into doing the same useless work. That's not working intelligently. It may feel safe, but it is not the best that you can do for you or for others. You won't be satisfied with setting your aim low. Therefore, raise your aim. Get curious about identifying worthwhile challenges and how you can help. By trying, you're working out the experience you want. Once upon a time I was in a job that required lots of writing. My performance was rated below the criterion. Through taking writing classes, I developed my ability to become a writer.

Curiosity is a survival skill. Did curiosity kill the cat, or did worry or sorrow kill the cat? "Curiosity killed the cat" was not the original form of the proverb. The original form is not commonly known or used, but it's "care killed the cat." This older version of the proverb goes back to at least the sixteenth century. The more precise advice is that worry kills. Curiosity is the life skill to employ to figure out how you can do something. Curiosity is the life skill that can serve you well when you need to uncover opportunities disguised as obstacles. Reflect again on the words spoken by Walter E. Cole: "We must look for opportunities in every difficulty instead of being paralyzed at the thought of the difficulty in every opportunity."

Having an inquisitive mind can ease you into quality problem solving and creative thinking. If asking questions doesn't come to you naturally, you are not alone. Many people have become socialized to believe that answers are more important than questions. You simply have to unlearn that bad habit. I trust the upcoming section will help you begin your successful transition toward being comfortable with and good at asking questions. If you are becoming enthusiastic or perhaps anxious about boosting your ability to become terrific at asking questions or developing creative thinking, I recommend you read *How to Think like Leonardo da Vinci* by Michael J. Gelb.

Developing questions that can trigger insightful answers requires spending time in contemplation. Sitting in moments of uncertainty does not feel good. It is natural to wish for quick solutions. Moving forward with bad ideas, however, will end you from the skillet into the fire. Consider this: Can you outrun the tiger? No. Does the tiger expect you to run? Yes. If you don't run, that might confuse the tiger. While the tiger is in a state of puzzlement, you might have enough time to contemplate an escape plan. The best possible outcome is the tiger senses you are not typical prey, so it simply retreats. Contemplating during moments of uncertainty at work or at home can help you discover answers that solve problems. With practice, you can make asking questions the starting point.

Michael J. Gelb organized some questions well suited for fact finding in his book just mentioned. Gelb is a world-renowned innovator in the fields of creative thinking, accelerated learning, and leadership. In the book, Gelb pointed out, "Most business innovations are inspired by the question what if…? The example he gave is, "asking the question what if we shrunk the computer chips swelled the economy of Silicon Valley." Since obstacles are simply opportunities in disguise, then perhaps the biggest opportunity obstacles give us is the chance for us to experience continuous learning."

The Questions for Fact Finding Organized by Michael J. Gelb:

- When   did it start? does it happen? will the consequences of it be felt? must it be resolved?
- Who   cares about it? is affected by it? created it? perpetuates it? can help solve it?
- How   does it happen? can I get more objective information? can I look at it from unfamiliar perspectives? can it be changed? will I know it has been solved?
- Where   does it happen? did it begin? haven't I looked? else has this happened?
- Why   is it important? did it start? does it continue?

Stay in the Arena

Fighting for what you want to see happen is also one way to work out the experience you want. Since the human inclination is to move toward things perceived as pleasurable and away from those perceived as painful, become keenly aware of when you are doing either of those. Realize that progress comes from meeting challenges, and pleasure derives from making progress. Jumping out of the arena to escape the pain before the gain goes against your best interest.

Have you ever asked the question of where challenges originate from? Challenges are part of life. A challenge can be human inspired. For instance, wanting to learn a foreign language is a human aspiration. My desire to write this book instigated a challenge—having to write the book. Every challenge, test, trial, and contest having to do with writing the book resulted from my aspiration to stretch to do something better and new—something I believed I ought to do. At the exact moment I made up my mind to present a book that contained my ideas for how to work joyfully, I caused a challenge to come into my life.

At the precise moment you wish to improve something about yourself or anything else, you create a personal challenge. Because tests and trials do not feel good, your human inclination to retreat will emerge. When it does, quiet the negative thoughts running through your head. That will enable you to sense the pleasures that will come from meeting the challenge and to stay inspired. Remember you created the idea to improve yourself or something else. The pleasures you sense can be yours if you stay in the arena and work your way to the other side.

In the arena, you will get knocked down. When that happens, critics will raise their voices against you. The twenty-sixth president of the United States, Theodore Roosevelt, indicated, "It is not the critic who counts, not the man who points out how the strong man stumbled, or where the doer of deeds could have done better. The credit belongs to the man who is actually in the arena, whose face is marred by dust and sweat and blood, who strives valiantly, who errs and comes up short again and again, who knows the great enthusiasms, the great devotions, and spends himself in a worthy cause, who at best knows achievement, and who at worst if he fails at least fails while daring greatly so that his place shall never be with those cold and timid souls who know neither victory or defeat."

Listen to Your Inner Voice and Use Your Imaginative Ability

To work out the experience you want, listen to your inner voice and use your imaginative ability. Two common definitions for inner voice are: It's a form of intuiting inspirational information, and it's listening to your higher self. Think of your inner voice as your best guide and dependable friend.

Imagination is the process of taking in information and forming new ideas. About the role of imagination in working out the experience you want: Everything is created from imagination. Through imagination, people fashion raw information into tools for improving lives. Having raw information without imagination is akin to knowing water quenches thirst but not being able to haul it out of the earth. That is likely what Albert Einstein meant when he said that "imagination is more important than knowledge."

Take into account the volumes of useful information floating around in heads, stored on computers, and scribbled on paper. Now imagine people mulling over the information and figuring out how to use it to improve society by enriching families, communities, and organizations. Are you sensing the enormity of the good possibilities? Are you seeing the role of inner voice as extremely important?

When I read about CNN's 2015 hero of the year Maggie Doyne, I saw her as a role model of trusting the inner voice and acting on the images and sensations perceived. I decided to write about then-eighteen-year-old Maggie Doyne of New Jersey. She changed the world of the women and children in the remote village of Surkhet, Nepal. Maggie said, "If we all had the attitude that we can do anything, that we can be anything, if we follow our dreams and our hearts…we can change the world."

By all accounts, her work and the BlinkNow Foundation she established to sustain that work are the outcomes of listening to her inner voice and using her imagination to fashion raw information into resources. As you read Maggie's story, I ask you to wonder something. How is it that within ten years she could go from being an eighteen-year-old high school graduate to being CNN's 2015 hero of the year? Consider what parts went into the production of the works she produced for the children and women of Nepal.

Before you move on to Maggie's story, please take into your heart a few gifts from her wrapped in quotation marks.

- "Love yourself and feel your power. We all are capable of so much more than we ever imagine."
- "Follow your heart. Do what you love. For any problem, education is usually the answer."
- "We believe that in the blink of an eye, we can all make a difference."

In high school, Maggie's eyes were fixed on nothing but starting college. At the last moment, though, she changed her mind. Realizing that attending college would be a huge investment of time and money, she concluded that she needed to first figure out what she wanted to do, who she wanted to be, and where she wanted to go. As she stated in an interview, "I needed to know what's on the inside of me a little more. I thought maybe then I could make that kind of commitment." She went on to say, "It was a rite of passage that

I wanted, that I was looking for…I think we've lost that in our culture, that intersection, in-between time because we're all so focused on the next thing, on looking externally, always outside ourselves."

With no particular plans other than to explore the world for one year before starting college, Maggie headed east. She spent time in a Buddhist monastery and helped with the construction of a seawall off the island nation of Fiji. Four months later, she landed in India. What happened next shifted the course of her life. She found herself in the war-torn and poverty-stricken villages of Nepal.

While spending some time in India working with Nepalese refugees from Nepal's decade-long civil war, she met a young girl who wanted to find her family in Nepal. As in all war-torn countries, women and children were suffering the most. That was what Maggie observed in Nepal, and that was what inspired her to call her parents and ask them to wire her the $5,000 she had earned babysitting. With that money, she purchased land in Surkhet, a district in western Nepal. She worked with the local community there for two years to build the Kopila Valley Children's Home, which opened in 2007. Kopila means "flower bud" in Nepali.

Maggie's provision of community services to the children and women of Surkhet, Nepal, grew a lot in a decade. In 2010 the Kopila Valley School opened to address high rates of illiteracy, school dropouts, and unemployment. With the demand for higher education and the promise of job security brought on by the postwar economic development, the school served to close the relational gap between education and opportunity.

Maggie's work in the remote village of Surkhet continued in 2011, the year that the Kopila Valley Health Clinic opened. As Maggie pointed out, "They realized that kids wouldn't attend [school] regularly or be able to succeed until they were healthy and nourished—and that they wouldn't be healthy and nourished until they came to school." According to Maggie, "Creating an environment where children thrive and succeed really is like solving a puzzle… health and education goes together like two pieces of a puzzle."

Maggie and her team continued to turn their dreams into realities. In 2013 they opened the doors to the Kopila Valley Women's Center on the premise and promise that amazing things would happen when women came together to support each other. Their confidence in women brings to mind this teaching of the Baha'i faith: "The world of humanity is possessed of two wings: the male and the female. So long as these two wings are not equivalent in strength, the bird will not fly...When the two wings...become equivalent in strength, enjoying the same prerogatives, the flight of man will be exceedingly lofty and extraordinary."

The purpose of the Kopila Valley Women's Center was to provide life-changing job training and education to women in the Surkhet community. In 2014 the team connected two aspects of the women's center. To expand, a retail shop was included in town. Graduates of their training program staffed the store, and the women's beautiful handmade products stocked it. In addition, they expanded to include a counseling center and a microloan program.

Maggie and her team also set the stage to link sustainability and growth in the Kopila Valley community. The international movement for sustainability is about creating a world in which the environment does not need protecting. One element of the Kopila Valley community sustainability program is the large garden. This supplies healthy organic fruits and vegetables to their school lunch program, which serves more than four hundred hot meals each day. They compost what is not used. They source rice that they cook every day from nearby farms. Solar panels and biogas are used to keep the carbon footprint of the children's home and the school low. The children and students are being taught how to live sustainably and to share knowledge about important environmental issues.

The strong feelings Maggie had about using a year before college to discover her passion for life and sticking with that theme once she found herself in the Surkhet community of Nepal were simply representations of her tremendous courage and commitment to her true self. She believes, "It's not about putting on a backpack and going somewhere. It's about living with kindness. We need more compassion, and we need it everywhere. What matters is how you live. It's about making the most loving, conscious choices you can every day."

In her acceptance speech for CNN's 2015 Hero of the Year award, she said, "And to all of you in this room and who are watching, please, please remember that we have the power to create the world that we want to live in, just as we want it. And that's what all the heroes here tonight have done." Maggie established the BlinkNow Foundation to sustain, grow, and support Kopila Valley Children's Home and Kopila Valley School in Nepal. She said, "At BlinkNow we believe in a blink of an eye, we all can make a difference… We believe that every child in the world should be provided with the most basic needs and rights—a safe home, medical care, education, and love. And with that, they can grow up to be adults with a social conscience and the skills to continue our mission of ending the cycle of poverty and violence in our world."

Maggie's story is touching because combining making a living and re-sourcefulness to make good things happen affects you. As Maggie said, "It's not about putting on a backpack and going somewhere—it it's about living with kindness."

Living with kindness, listening to his inner voice, and using his imaginative ability are the things causing Joe Seals, head custodian at Thalia Elementary in Virginia Beach, Virginia, to have a positive impact on kids. Kids' opinions of Mr. Seals reveal why he was given the NewsChannel 3 People Taking Action Award. According to fifth grader Jaylen Harris, "He always makes sure you're feeling good when you're on a bad day." Lilly Moore said, "He's always there. Whenever you're down or doubtful, he'll be just like making you feel better." To Delancey Moore, Seals is part of the family. Delancey said, "It's kinda like a big brother, how he acts is like a big brother to me." Principal Pamela Pastros's description of Mr. Seals tells more about his giving. She said, "If they need something to stay warm—he's going to find them a coat, mittens, gloves… things of that nature." After twenty-seven years, Mr. Seals could have easily slipped into doing the same old thing. Principal Pastros said, "He's been here so long he doesn't see himself as the custodian, because he's not just a custodi-an, he does anything and everything around this building." What drives him? Mr. Seals said, "Well, I just want to say thank God and thank these lovable children, because without them, I wouldn't be here and I love helping them."

His motivation for doing all the things he does for the students is based on what he said: "From the heart…because I was a kid—there was someone who had to listen to what I had to say."

While working nearly a decade as a sales consultant at a retail home furnishing company, my inner voice guided me right. Exceeding many sales-category goals, learning the ropes, serving customers, and assisting struggling sales consultants fulfilled me. I have lots of tender memories. Former co-worker John Wilson gave me this one: "When I first began working at The Dump [furniture store] I had no sales experience whatsoever and felt very uncertain about my ability to succeed in the field. The very first day of work Alice came up to our new hire group, introduced herself, welcomed us to the sales floor, and offered to assist us in learning the ropes in any way she could. I sensed that her offer was sincere and in the ensuing months that proved to be the case. No matter how busy she was, Alice always made time to answer our questions, assist us with learning to use the archaic computer system we had, and boost our flagging confidence when she noticed we needed some encouragement. She even went so far as to share customers with us, a gesture that is unheard of in straight-commission sales work—I credit the fact that I made it through the nerve-racking few months of learning sales to Alice's caring mentorship and unselfish team-building approach to sharing the sales floor."

Eight

PERSONAL MOTIVATIONS AND PREFERENCES FOR WORK

The calling is to serve you so you can serve others. So my proposal to you is this: work on yourself more than you do on your job. I hope that by reviewing explanations for each of the nine elements in this chapter, you can build on your sense of what else to do to win the battle of making your work journey sweeter. The more prepared you are to handle the drudgeries of work, the more prepared you are to defeat the chance of not satisfying your innate desire to make good things happen.

Element: Interest in the Job Content

Interest in the job content is about those tasks you want to perform. Tasks you want to perform make up your true motivations and preferences. Once you are aware of your true motivations and preferences toward work, you are ready to move on to matching them to jobs out there. It is safe for you to assume that your true motivations and preferences are based on what you want to do, what you're most likely drawn to do, what you're willing to do often, what you will sacrifice to train to do, and what you want to transform from raw interest into reality.

Element: Temperament for the Job

Once you have identified tasks you want to perform, the next important step is to classify your temperament for the job. Temperament is how you prefer to perform tasks. That is how temperament for the job and interest in the job differ. Both are based on motivations and preferences, however. Say you have motivations and preferences for change and variety in the job. That is an element of your temperament. Another way for you to understand temperament is to think of it as the prevailing or dominant quality of your mind that characterizes you. There is no right or wrong or bad or good when it comes to temperament for the job. It is important for you to identify how you prefer to perform tasks. Do you prefer to do work in teams or independently? Do you prefer to work under the management or supervision of others, or do you prefer to plan, control, and direct activities of others?

Element: Aptitude for the Job

Aptitude for the job is about your natural tendency to do something well—especially something that can be further developed. Once you have a good sense of your best talents and skills, the next step is to look out into the world of work and fit them where they would function best with your interest in the job.

Element: People

Knowing your motivations and preferences for interacting with people in the work world is also important. Low motivation for people-intensive jobs is perfectly fine if your job necessitates or requires you to function apart from others, manage your own activities, or be satisfied with working in isolation. It's vital for you to know what you prefer and what you have the natural tendency to do and develop within you.

Element: Things

Knowing how you relate to things is of great consequence too. "Things" includes but is not limited to management of materials and processes and knowledge of operational and mechanical forces or objects. Knowing if you have a natural mechanical savvy is essential too.

Element: Data

The way in which you relate to data is based on the kinds of mental activities you are motivated to engage in. Such mental activities are primarily intellectual, academic, scholarly, scientific, mathematical, or professional. Say you prefer engaging in intellectual or philosophical mental activities. You might be more inclined, then, to relate to data for synthesizing—putting two or more things together to form a whole, combining separated elements of thoughts into a whole, or uniting divided parts. But you might not be inclined to relate to data for the purpose of teaching algebra.

Element: Reasoning

Suppose ten people were considering the same information. The where, why, and how they would apply to the same information depends on each person's priority for the information. The big-picture person's priority would more likely be to apply thinking toward uncovering patterns in complex problems, to come up with new ideas and new projects, and to outline what needs to be done. The detailed thinker's priority would more likely be to apply thinking toward considering things in great detail, paying excellent attention to details, editing or tweaking a plan, and executing the details of a plan or project.

Element: Mathematical Capacity

Math is everywhere. It is safe to say everyone uses math, and everyone has some degree of interest in math. How you relate to the applied usage of math is based on the vocational interest you have. Most likely, the mathematical capacity you develop will also be based on the vocational interest you have. For example, if one of the interests you have for the applied usage of math is for tracking, analyzing, and proving business activities and performance, then that is one of your motivational factors for learning, working with, using, and applying mathematics.

Element: Language Capacity

Language is the use of words. Everyone applies language in his or her profession. Appreciating how you relate to the applied usage of language is important. Is your interest in words a factor of literary, journalistic, or communicative activities?

"Literary" means related to literature, which encompasses books and writings published on a particular subject. "Journalistic" relates to journalism, which is the activity of gathering, assessing, creating, and presenting information. "Communicative" activities are those in which the aim is to encourage people to speak and listen to others, find information, break down barriers, and talk about themselves.

The reward of living your personal motivations and preferences for work is a lot of inner satisfaction and professional respect. That is exactly what American professional baseball player Babe Ruth got to experience when he stopped pitching in order to focus on batting. He knew he had the motivation to be a great batter. Even though he had become a stellar left-handed pitcher, he achieved his greatest fame as a slugging outfielder. It is important to appreciate that he took a lot of criticism for his decision, but he lived his personal motivation and preferences in the world of baseball.

Nine

WORK AND A HEALTHY RELATIONSHIP WITH THE SELF

You can achieve much for you and others by building and maintaining a healthy relationship with the self. Live the spiritual teaching that tells us, "To thine own self be true." Be true to you, trust in you, and believe in you. Don't dismiss your inner urges. The answer to whether you ought to go left or right should come from you only. People can cheer you on in your decision, but they are not able to make better decisions for you than you can.

Who has the ability to know you better than you? Perhaps that was what Henry David Thoreau meant when he said, "It is what a man thinks of himself that really determines his fate." According to Galileo Galilei, "You cannot teach a man anything…You can only help him find it within himself."

A month after my mother-in-law, Beatrice Bing, departed this life on January 29, 2000 she spoke to me through my dream. She emphasized the wise thinking of Thoreau and Galilei in how she answered my question to her. I asked, "Mom, do you have something you want to tell me?" Her answer was, "Everything you need to know is inside you." Her answer granted me the permission I needed to place a lot of trust in my gut feeling of how I should present my inner self in all facets of the physical world. I'm passing on to you the permission she gave to me.

Trusting my gut is how I came to be a self-made person of facilitation of joy of working. I was not able to substantiate ahead of time how I was going to make that happen. The education I received through earning the Bachelor of Science degree with the major speech communications from Florida State University supported my aim to persuade workers to make firm their steps toward having fulfilling workdays. Speech communication is a program that focuses on the scientific, humanistic, and critical study of human communication in a variety of formats, media, and contexts. It includes instruction in the theory and practice of interpersonal, group, organizational, professional, and intercultural communication; speaking and listening; verbal and nonverbal interaction; rhetorical theory and criticism; performance studies; argumentation and persuasion; technologically mediated communication; popular culture; and various contextual applications.

The training was excellent. However I accomplished becoming a joy of work influencer through determination, discipline, and by following virtues such as the ones suggested by Benjamin Franklin who was one of the Founding Fathers of the United States. A renowned polymath, Franklin was a leading author, printer, political theorist, politician, freemason, postmaster, scientist, inventor, civic activist, statesman, and diplomat.

Virtues of a self-made person as suggested by Benjamin Franklin:

- Being motivated to accomplish the goal
- Surrounding self with people who have the same mindset and goals as you
- Learning from others who have become self-made people and being able to take advice from them
- Using silence, order, and moderation to develop characteristics that are needed to become a self-made person

A healthy relationship with the self is rooted in being true to you. Trust in the special ability you have to know something that cannot be verified ahead of time. Think back to the story of Maggie Doyne in chapter 5. I regard Maggie's story as a perfect example of knowing something that cannot be verified ahead of time and of the importance of a healthy relationship with the self.

Transformational life coach Chérie Carter-Scott, PhD, eloquently conveys the importance of the relationship with the self. In *Transformational Life Coaching: Creating Limitless Opportunities for Yourself and Others,* she wrote, "Your relationship with yourself is the central template from which your personal destiny manifests. The relationship with the self is the most important and crucial relationship in your life. Your career, your personal relationships, your home, and your health are all a direct result of the quality of your relationship with you. The way you hold yourself creates a vibration that sends a message to the world about who you are, what you deserve, and how you should be treated. The relationship with the self is the way you hold, perceive, believe in, and relate to you." Another statement from her book is this: "When you do what you say, and make your words count, you are operating with integrity." She provided this perspective of integrity: "Integrity comes from the Latin word that means whole. Integrity means that you are undivided and adhere to your principles and standards even when it is inconvenient. When you operate with integrity, you are aligned with your highest aspirations of yourself."

Because participation in gossiping is a sure way to block having a healthy relationship with self and others, I decided to write about consultation as a means for restoring and maintaining a healthy relationship with you and others. I'm convinced the cure to gossiping is a person's motivation to infuse attributes of consultation into conversations. Choosing to learn about the benefits of consultation and moving on to learn how to ease self and others into consultation is making an intelligent decision.

Here are some attributes of gossip published widely:

- Synonyms for gossip are scoop, buzz, water-cooler talk, and latest news.
- Gossip acts as though it is an agent for relationship building and bonding.
- Gossiping's sole intent is to harm by unnecessarily revealing personal details of other people's lives, whether those details are rumor or fact.
- Gossiping involves discussing the faults of others, in their absence, with the intent to make them look bad.

- Gossiping involves saying things that doesn't enhance the person spoken about, the listener, or the speaker.
- Gossiping reduces the sender and the receiver to mere junkies.

Here are some motivations to gossip published widely:

- to belong,
- to fit in,
- to be a go-to person,
- to cover up personal miseries,
- to feel more worthy, and
- to be entertained.

Here are attributes of consultation by way of the Baha'i faith

- Consultation bestows greater awareness and transmutes speculation into certainty.
- Consultation is a shining light leading the way in dark situations.
- Consultation creates a station of perfection and maturity.
- Consultation manifests understanding.
- Consultation facilitates individual investigation of truth.
- Consultation induces an attitude, a will, and an aspiration toward discovery and implementation of practical measures.

Here are some motivations to choose consultation by way of the Baha'i faith:

- has regard for a person's interests and needs,
- has a desire to be attached only to the best,
- has a desire to facilitate helpfulness,
- has a desire to foster harmony between people,
- has a desire to forget personalities,
- has a desire to resist the temptation to take sides, and
- has a desire to be free from entanglement.

Ten

ERECTING CELEBRATORY RITUALS FOR WORK

A ritual is a religious or solemn ceremony consisting of a series of actions performed according to a prescribed order. Common actions are sequences of activities involving gestures, words, and objects and performed in a set-aside place according to set sequences. Rituals may be prescribed by the traditions of a community, such as standing and placing the hand over the heart before pledging allegiance to the US flag. A common ritual in religious communities is closing one's eyes during the presentation of a prayer. The purpose of rituals is to maximize one's ability to focus on and remember the most important things of life.

Negative aspects of work can distract us from answering the ancient calling pertaining to work. Here are some methods that might increase your ability to pay attention to the most important things of work. As a rule say "thanks". It's an easy way to inspire working people and to stay concentrated on positive aspects of work. I like giving the "OK" hand sign especially to school bus drivers, road workers, custodians, trash collectors, maids, and persons serving in jobs our society fail to properly appreciate.

I adore a produce section stocked with the freshest of fruits and vegetables. So I thank produce clerks for helping to make my buying and eating experience pleasing. Saluting is another gesture I make to say I appreciate the thoughtful ways you do that job.

When reading or hearing about someone working in the spirit of service, I say "all right", "great job", "I love it", or "wonderful". Social media has provided me endless opportunities to do that. Try my methods or come up with your own. The point is to allow your mind to enjoy the constructive qualities of work. To focus on the helpful things you're turning out, congratulate you. For working competently, virtuously, imaginatively, or the likes of such, say "great job", give the "thumb up", say "I did it".

Work is one of those parts of life that has its share of difficulties. You have to do everything possible to make work a fulfilling life event. It's a long journey to undertake displeased.

These are some positive aspects of work:

- station for serving you and others,
- place for facilitating change,
- surplus of professionalism,
- place for taking initiative,
- diverse viewpoints,
- group work,
- imagination at work, and
- social interactions.

Conclusion

Because so much that is required for us to have wholesome lives are rooted in working, it's no wonder the calling is to make a difference in the world through occupations. It is incumbent on each of us to discover the type of satisfaction that can come only from working in the spirit of service. It is the obligation of each individual to find comfort in causing human affairs to improve and communities to flourish. It is the responsibility of every working person to become the king of something.

All it takes to make a difference is the desire of one person to take greater responsibility for doing work that moves the world along. How much and how well we progress collectively depends on the extent to which each person is excited about working to get what is needed and give what is needed.

How can we overcome the greatest of human challenges? We can start by elevating our thoughts and actions above situations that easily beset our best intentions and abilities. Each person can begin the process of change by refuting every fantasized notion of the purpose of work. Let each of us hasten to adhere to the ancient calling pertaining to work. Let each of us also find pleasure in being the person working to give what helps. Tiny pushes from each honest worker can move human affairs from good to great. Let none of us come under the influence of drudgeries of work. Let each of us work on becoming a good manager of uncovering opportunities disguised as difficulties. Let us be mindful of the purpose of the world of work to serve as a great gathering of helpers.

About the Author

Alice Elizabeth Bing has been a Joy of Working consultant since 2005. She runs speaking events and conferences and processes the trademarked MAPP career assessment for students, graduates, and working adults. The trajectory of her career journey was from community organizer, volunteer manager, supervisor, community relations manager, fund development manager, sales consultant, and substitute teacher to owner of the Working Joyfully Consulting Group.

Her current residence is in Virginia Beach, Virginia, with her husband, Moses Lee Bing. Enjoying the goodness of faith, family, friends, and fun is another passion of hers. Contact her at abing@thewjcgroup.com.

www.ingramcontent.com/pod-product-compliance
Lightning Source LLC
Chambersburg PA
CBHW070940180526
45168CB00003B/1119